50 Kid Adventure Recipes for Home

By: Kelly Johnson

Table of Contents

- Trail Mix
- Banana Boats
- Camping Quesadillas
- Campfire Cones
- Foil Packet Meals (with various ingredients)
- Campfire Pizza
- Walking Tacos
- Campfire Popcorn
- S'mores Dip
- Campfire Breadsticks
- Campfire Cinnamon Rolls
- Grilled Cheese Sandwiches
- Fruit Kabobs
- Veggie Skewers
- Campfire Nachos
- Pita Pizzas
- Campfire Sausage and Veggie Foil Packets
- Campfire Corn on the Cob
- Campfire Hot Dogs
- Campfire Baked Beans
- Grilled Pineapple Slices
- Grilled Peach Halves
- Grilled Watermelon Slices
- Foil Packet Fish
- Campfire Chicken Fajitas
- Campfire Meatball Subs
- Campfire Chili
- Campfire Mac and Cheese
- Campfire Breakfast Burritos
- Pancake Skewers
- Grilled Peanut Butter and Jelly Sandwiches
- Campfire Stuffed Peppers
- Campfire Chicken Wings
- Campfire Sausage and Potato Hash
- Campfire Breakfast Hash

- Campfire French Toast
- Campfire Cereal Bars
- Campfire Banana Splits
- Campfire Cobbler
- Campfire Rice Krispie Treats
- Campfire Apple Crisp
- Campfire Peach Melba
- Campfire Bread Pudding
- Campfire Monkey Bread
- Campfire Tacos in a Bag
- Campfire Pasta Salad
- Campfire Caesar Salad
- Campfire Grilled Vegetables
- Campfire Sausage and Egg Breakfast Burritos
- Campfire Chicken and Rice Casserole

Trail Mix

Ingredients:

- 1 cup nuts (such as almonds, peanuts, cashews, walnuts, or a mix)
- 1 cup seeds (such as sunflower seeds, pumpkin seeds, or a mix)
- 1 cup dried fruit (such as raisins, cranberries, apricots, mango, pineapple, or a mix)
- 1 cup pretzels, broken into pieces
- 1 cup chocolate chips, M&M's, or other small candies (optional)
- 1 cup cereal (such as Cheerios, Chex, or granola)
- 1/2 teaspoon salt (optional, if using unsalted nuts)
- Spices or seasonings to taste (such as cinnamon, nutmeg, or cocoa powder, optional)

Instructions:

1. Prepare the ingredients:
    - If using large nuts, chop them into smaller pieces if desired.
    - If using large dried fruit, chop them into smaller pieces if desired.
2. Combine the ingredients:
    - In a large mixing bowl, combine all the ingredients together.
    - Mix well to ensure that the ingredients are evenly distributed.
3. Store the trail mix:
    - Transfer the trail mix to an airtight container or resealable bags.
    - Store in a cool, dry place until ready to enjoy.
4. Customize:
    - Feel free to customize the trail mix according to your preferences. You can adjust the quantities of each ingredient or add additional ingredients such as coconut flakes, chocolate-covered nuts or fruit, popcorn, or small crackers.
5. Enjoy:
    - Trail mix is ready to enjoy as a snack on the go, a quick energy boost during hikes or outdoor activities, or a tasty treat any time of day!

Trail mix is highly customizable, so feel free to experiment with different combinations of nuts, seeds, dried fruits, and other ingredients to create your perfect snack mix.

Banana Boats

Ingredients:

- Ripe bananas (1 per serving)
- Chocolate chips
- Mini marshmallows
- Optional toppings: chopped nuts, shredded coconut, sprinkles, caramel sauce, peanut butter chips, or any other toppings you like

Instructions:

1. Prepare the bananas:
    - Leave the peel on the bananas and make a lengthwise slit down the center, cutting through the peel and just into the banana flesh (but not all the way through). Make sure not to cut through the bottom peel.
2. Fill the banana:
    - Stuff the slit in the banana with chocolate chips and mini marshmallows, alternating between the two until the banana is filled. You can also add any additional toppings you like at this point.
3. Wrap in foil:
    - Wrap each stuffed banana tightly in aluminum foil, leaving a little room at the top for steam to escape.
4. Cook over the campfire:
    - Place the foil-wrapped banana boats on the grate over the campfire or on hot coals. Cook for about 5-10 minutes, or until the chocolate and marshmallows are melted and the bananas are soft and caramelized.
5. Serve:
    - Carefully unwrap the foil from the banana boats.
    - Serve the warm banana boats with spoons and enjoy the gooey, chocolaty, marshmallowy goodness straight from the peel!

Banana boats are a versatile treat, so feel free to get creative with the fillings and toppings. You can also experiment with adding different flavors of chocolate chips, using different types of nuts, or drizzling with sauces for extra flavor. Enjoy this delicious campfire dessert on your next outdoor adventure!

Camping Quesadillas

Ingredients:

- Flour tortillas
- Shredded cheese (such as cheddar, Monterey Jack, or a Mexican cheese blend)
- Cooked chicken, beef, or beans (optional)
- Sliced vegetables (such as bell peppers, onions, or mushrooms)
- Salsa, guacamole, sour cream, or other desired toppings (optional)

Instructions:

1. Prepare your ingredients:
    - If you're using cooked meat or beans, make sure they are cooked and ready to go. You can prepare them ahead of time or use leftovers from a previous meal.
    - Slice any vegetables you plan to use and have them ready to go.
2. Assemble the quesadillas:
    - Place one tortilla on a flat surface.
    - Sprinkle a layer of shredded cheese evenly over half of the tortilla.
    - If using, add your desired fillings such as cooked meat, beans, or sliced vegetables on top of the cheese.
    - Sprinkle another layer of cheese over the fillings.
    - Fold the tortilla in half to cover the fillings and form a half-moon shape.
3. Cook over the campfire:
    - Heat a cast-iron skillet or a grill pan over the campfire or camping stove.
    - Place the assembled quesadilla in the hot skillet and cook for a few minutes on each side, until the tortilla is golden brown and crispy and the cheese is melted.
    - If you don't have a skillet, you can also cook the quesadilla directly on a grate over the campfire, using tongs to flip it halfway through cooking.
4. Serve:
    - Once the quesadilla is cooked to your liking, remove it from the skillet and let it cool for a minute or two.
    - Use a sharp knife or pizza cutter to cut the quesadilla into wedges.
    - Serve the warm quesadilla wedges with your favorite toppings such as salsa, guacamole, sour cream, or any other desired condiments.

Camping quesadillas are a versatile meal that you can customize with your favorite ingredients. They're perfect for a quick and satisfying dinner after a day of outdoor adventure!

Campfire Cones

Ingredients:

- Ice cream cones (sugar cones or waffle cones work well)
- Assorted fillings/toppings (choose from options like chocolate chips, mini marshmallows, sliced bananas, berries, peanut butter chips, caramel sauce, nuts, sprinkles, or any other desired fillings)

Instructions:

1. Prepare your ingredients:
    - Set out a variety of fillings and toppings in small bowls or containers. Get creative and choose a selection that you and your fellow campers will enjoy.
2. Assemble the campfire cones:
    - Take a piece of aluminum foil and place a cone on top.
    - Fill the cone with your desired fillings and toppings, layering them as you like. Make sure to leave some space at the top of the cone to prevent spillage.
    - You can mix and match different fillings and toppings to create a variety of flavors.
3. Wrap in foil:
    - Carefully wrap each filled cone in aluminum foil, making sure to seal the edges tightly.
4. Cook over the campfire:
    - Place the foil-wrapped cones on a grate over the campfire or directly on hot coals.
    - Cook for about 5-10 minutes, turning occasionally, until the fillings are melted and gooey and the cone is warm and slightly crispy.
5. Serve:
    - Carefully unwrap the foil from the cones.
    - Enjoy the warm and gooey campfire cones straight from the foil, using a spoon or simply holding them by the cone.
    - Be careful, as the filling may be hot!

Campfire cones are a fun and customizable dessert that's sure to be a hit with kids and adults alike. They're easy to make and require minimal cleanup, making them perfect for outdoor gatherings or camping trips. Enjoy experimenting with different fillings and toppings to create your perfect campfire cone!

Foil Packet Meals (with various ingredients)

Ingredients:

- Protein: Choose from options like chicken, beef, shrimp, fish, tofu, or sausage.
- Vegetables: Use a variety of fresh or frozen vegetables such as bell peppers, onions, zucchini, carrots, potatoes, broccoli, or corn.
- Seasonings: Use your favorite herbs, spices, and sauces to flavor the meal. Options include garlic, Italian seasoning, lemon pepper, barbecue sauce, soy sauce, or teriyaki sauce.
- Olive oil or butter: For adding moisture and flavor to the ingredients.

Instructions:

1. Prepare the ingredients:
    - Cut the protein and vegetables into bite-sized pieces, if necessary.
    - Season the protein and vegetables with your desired herbs, spices, and sauces. Toss them in a bowl with olive oil or melted butter to coat evenly.
2. Assemble the foil packets:
    - Tear off sheets of heavy-duty aluminum foil, large enough to wrap around the ingredients and create a sealed packet.
    - Place a portion of the seasoned protein and vegetables in the center of each foil sheet.
3. Wrap and seal the packets:
    - Bring the two long sides of the foil together over the ingredients and fold them down to meet the food.
    - Fold the edges of the foil over several times to create a tight seal, leaving a little room for steam to circulate inside.
4. Cook over the campfire or grill:
    - Preheat the grill or set up a campfire with hot coals.
    - Place the foil packets directly on the grill grates or on a grate over the campfire.
    - Cook for about 10-20 minutes, depending on the thickness of the protein and the type of vegetables used. Flip the packets halfway through cooking to ensure even cooking.
5. Check for doneness:

- Carefully open one foil packet to check if the protein is cooked through and the vegetables are tender. Be cautious of hot steam when opening the packets.
6. Serve:
    - Once the foil packets are cooked to your liking, carefully remove them from the grill or campfire.
    - Open the packets carefully to avoid steam burns.
    - Serve the contents directly from the foil packets or transfer them to plates.
    - Enjoy your delicious and hassle-free foil packet meal!

Foil packet meals are versatile and can be customized with a wide variety of ingredients to suit your taste preferences. They're perfect for camping trips, cookouts, or anytime you want a quick and easy meal with minimal cleanup.

Campfire Pizza

Ingredients:

- Pizza dough (you can use store-bought or homemade dough)
- Pizza sauce
- Shredded mozzarella cheese
- Toppings of your choice (such as pepperoni, sliced bell peppers, onions, mushrooms, olives, cooked sausage, or any other desired toppings)
- Olive oil
- Cornmeal or flour (for dusting)

Instructions:

1. Prepare the pizza dough:
    - If using store-bought dough, follow the package instructions to let it come to room temperature.
    - If making homemade dough, prepare the dough according to your favorite recipe and let it rise until doubled in size.
2. Prepare the toppings:
    - While the dough is rising, prepare your desired pizza toppings. Slice any vegetables and cook any meats that need to be cooked before assembling the pizza.
3. Prepare the campfire:
    - Build a campfire and let it burn down to hot coals. You'll need a good bed of hot coals to cook the pizza.
4. Assemble the pizza:
    - Dust a flat surface or a cutting board with cornmeal or flour to prevent the dough from sticking.
    - Stretch or roll out the pizza dough into your desired shape and thickness.
    - Brush one side of the dough with olive oil to prevent sticking to the grill grate.
5. Cook the pizza:
    - Carefully transfer the oiled side of the dough onto a clean and lightly greased grill grate placed over the hot coals.
    - Cook the dough for a few minutes, until it starts to firm up and develop grill marks on the bottom.
6. Add the toppings:

- Flip the dough over using tongs or a spatula.
- Spread pizza sauce evenly over the cooked side of the dough.
- Sprinkle shredded mozzarella cheese over the sauce, followed by your desired toppings.

7. Finish cooking:
   - Cover the grill with a lid or a large piece of aluminum foil to help the cheese melt and the toppings cook.
   - Cook the pizza for a few more minutes, until the cheese is melted and bubbly and the crust is cooked through and crispy.

8. Serve:
   - Carefully remove the pizza from the grill using tongs or a spatula.
   - Transfer the pizza to a cutting board and let it cool for a minute or two before slicing.
   - Slice the pizza into wedges or squares and serve hot.

Campfire pizza is a fun and versatile meal that you can customize with your favorite toppings. It's a great way to enjoy pizza in the great outdoors!

Walking Tacos

Ingredients:

- Individual-sized bags of corn chips (such as Fritos or Doritos)
- Cooked taco meat (ground beef or turkey seasoned with taco seasoning)
- Shredded lettuce
- Diced tomatoes
- Shredded cheese (such as cheddar or Mexican blend)
- Diced onions (optional)
- Sliced jalapeños (optional)
- Sour cream
- Salsa
- Guacamole or diced avocado
- Hot sauce (optional)

Instructions:

1. Prepare the taco meat:
   - In a skillet, cook the ground beef or turkey over medium heat until browned and cooked through.
   - Drain any excess fat and add taco seasoning according to package instructions. Stir to combine and simmer for a few minutes until the flavors meld together.
2. Prepare the toppings:
   - Chop and prepare all the toppings you plan to use, such as lettuce, tomatoes, onions, jalapeños, cheese, sour cream, salsa, guacamole, and hot sauce. Arrange them in individual bowls or containers for easy assembly.
3. Assemble the walking tacos:
   - Open the individual-sized bags of corn chips and crush them slightly to create a base for the tacos.
   - Add a spoonful of cooked taco meat on top of the crushed chips.
   - Layer on your desired toppings, such as lettuce, tomatoes, cheese, onions, jalapeños, sour cream, salsa, guacamole, and hot sauce.
4. Mix and enjoy:
   - Use a fork or spoon to mix all the ingredients together inside the bag until well combined.

- Eat the walking taco straight out of the bag with a fork or spoon.
- Enjoy the delicious combination of flavors and textures with each bite!

Walking tacos are completely customizable, so feel free to adjust the toppings according to your preferences. They're a fun and convenient way to enjoy tacos anywhere, anytime!

Campfire Popcorn

Ingredients:

- Popcorn kernels
- Vegetable oil or coconut oil
- Salt or other seasonings (optional)

Equipment:

- Heavy-duty aluminum foil
- Long-handled popcorn popper or a large pot with a lid
- Heat-resistant gloves or oven mitts

Instructions:

1. Prepare the popcorn kernels:
    - Measure out the desired amount of popcorn kernels. You'll need about 1/4 to 1/2 cup of kernels per batch, depending on how much popcorn you want to make.
2. Prepare the popcorn popper:
    - If you're using a long-handled popcorn popper, attach it securely to the handle.
    - If you're using a large pot with a lid, make sure the pot is clean and dry.
3. Prepare the foil packet:
    - Tear off a large piece of heavy-duty aluminum foil, about 2 feet long.
    - Place the popcorn kernels in the center of the foil.
4. Add oil and seasonings:
    - Drizzle a small amount of vegetable oil or coconut oil over the popcorn kernels. You'll need about 1 to 2 tablespoons of oil for each 1/4 cup of popcorn kernels.
    - Sprinkle salt or other seasonings over the kernels, if desired. You can also add seasonings like garlic powder, chili powder, or nutritional yeast for extra flavor.
5. Fold and seal the foil packet:
    - Fold the foil over the popcorn kernels to create a tight packet.
    - Fold the edges of the foil over several times to seal the packet completely, leaving a little room for steam to escape.

6. Cook over the campfire:
   - Hold the foil packet securely with heat-resistant gloves or oven mitts.
   - Place the foil packet directly on the hot coals of the campfire.
   - Shake the packet occasionally to ensure even cooking and to prevent burning.
7. Listen for popping sounds:
   - As the popcorn kernels heat up, they will start to pop. Listen for the popping sounds to gauge when the popcorn is ready.
8. Remove from the campfire:
   - Once the popping slows down significantly, carefully remove the foil packet from the campfire using heat-resistant gloves or oven mitts.
9. Open the foil packet:
   - Allow the foil packet to cool for a minute or two before carefully opening it.
   - Be cautious of hot steam when opening the packet.
10. Enjoy your campfire popcorn:
- Transfer the freshly popped popcorn to a bowl or serving container.
- Serve immediately and enjoy the warm and delicious campfire popcorn!

Campfire popcorn is a fun and tasty snack that's perfect for sharing around the campfire. Experiment with different seasonings and flavors to create your perfect batch of campfire popcorn!

S'mores Dip

Ingredients:

- 1 cup milk chocolate chips
- 1 cup mini marshmallows
- Graham crackers, for serving

Instructions:

1. Preheat the oven:
    - Preheat your oven to 350°F (175°C).
2. Prepare the baking dish:
    - Lightly grease a small oven-safe baking dish or skillet with butter or cooking spray.
3. Layer the chocolate chips:
    - Spread the milk chocolate chips evenly in the bottom of the prepared baking dish or skillet.
4. Add the marshmallows:
    - Scatter the mini marshmallows evenly over the chocolate chips, covering them completely.
5. Bake the dip:
    - Place the baking dish or skillet in the preheated oven and bake for about 10-15 minutes, or until the marshmallows are golden brown and toasted.
6. Serve:
    - Remove the dip from the oven and let it cool for a few minutes before serving.
    - Serve the s'mores dip warm, directly from the baking dish or skillet, with graham crackers for dipping.
7. Enjoy:
    - Use graham crackers to scoop up the gooey, melted chocolate and toasted marshmallows.
    - Enjoy the deliciousness of s'mores in dip form!

S'mores dip is a quick and easy dessert that's sure to be a hit at any gathering. You can also customize it by adding additional toppings such as chopped nuts, caramel sauce, or sprinkles. Serve it as a sweet treat for movie nights, game days, or any occasion where you want to indulge in a little bit of campfire nostalgia.

Campfire Breadsticks

Ingredients:

- 1 can refrigerated pizza dough or breadstick dough
- Olive oil or melted butter
- Garlic powder
- Italian seasoning
- Grated Parmesan cheese (optional)
- Marinara sauce or pizza sauce, for dipping (optional)

Instructions:

1. Prepare the campfire:
    - Build a campfire and let it burn down to hot coals. You'll need a bed of hot coals to cook the breadsticks.
2. Prepare the dough:
    - Open the can of refrigerated pizza dough or breadstick dough according to the package instructions.
    - If using pizza dough, divide it into strips about 1 inch wide. If using breadstick dough, separate it into individual breadsticks.
3. Season the dough:
    - Brush each strip of dough with olive oil or melted butter to coat evenly.
    - Sprinkle garlic powder and Italian seasoning over the oiled dough strips, to taste.
4. Cook over the campfire:
    - Carefully place the seasoned dough strips on a grate or skewers over the hot coals of the campfire.
    - Cook the breadsticks for about 5-10 minutes, turning occasionally, until they are golden brown and cooked through.
5. Serve:
    - Once the breadsticks are cooked to your liking, carefully remove them from the campfire.
    - Optionally, sprinkle grated Parmesan cheese over the hot breadsticks for extra flavor.
    - Serve the campfire breadsticks warm, with marinara sauce or pizza sauce for dipping, if desired.

Campfire breadsticks are a tasty and satisfying snack or side dish that's easy to make and enjoy outdoors. They're perfect for dipping into sauce or enjoying on their own as a savory treat around the campfire.

Campfire Cinnamon Rolls

Ingredients:

- 1 can refrigerated cinnamon roll dough
- Butter, softened
- Ground cinnamon
- Brown sugar
- Powdered sugar glaze (included with the cinnamon roll dough, or you can make your own)
- Optional toppings: chopped nuts, raisins, or dried fruit

Instructions:

1. Prepare the campfire:
    - Build a campfire and let it burn down to hot coals. You'll need a bed of hot coals to cook the cinnamon rolls.
2. Prepare the cinnamon roll dough:
    - Open the can of refrigerated cinnamon roll dough and separate the individual rolls.
    - Flatten each roll slightly with your hands or a rolling pin.
3. Fill the cinnamon rolls:
    - Spread a thin layer of softened butter over each flattened cinnamon roll.
    - Sprinkle ground cinnamon and brown sugar over the buttered dough, to taste.
    - Optionally, sprinkle chopped nuts, raisins, or dried fruit over the cinnamon sugar mixture.
4. Roll up the cinnamon rolls:
    - Roll each cinnamon roll into a tight spiral, starting from one end and rolling towards the other end.
5. Wrap in foil:
    - Tear off pieces of heavy-duty aluminum foil, large enough to wrap around each cinnamon roll individually.
    - Place each rolled cinnamon roll on a piece of foil and wrap it tightly, sealing the edges to prevent leakage.
6. Cook over the campfire:
    - Place the foil-wrapped cinnamon rolls on a grate or directly on hot coals of the campfire.

- Cook for about 10-15 minutes, turning occasionally, until the cinnamon rolls are golden brown and cooked through.
7. Glaze the cinnamon rolls:
    - Once the cinnamon rolls are cooked, carefully remove them from the campfire.
    - Drizzle the powdered sugar glaze over the hot cinnamon rolls while they are still warm.
8. Serve:
    - Serve the campfire cinnamon rolls warm, directly from the foil packets.
    - Enjoy the deliciousness of warm and gooey cinnamon rolls in the great outdoors!

Campfire cinnamon rolls are a delightful treat that's sure to be a hit with everyone around the campfire. They're easy to make and require minimal cleanup, making them perfect for outdoor adventures or cozy evenings under the stars.

Grilled Cheese Sandwiches

Ingredients:

- Bread slices (white, whole wheat, sourdough, or your favorite bread)
- Cheese slices or shredded cheese (cheddar, American, Swiss, provolone, or your favorite cheese)
- Butter or margarine, softened

Instructions:

1. Prepare the ingredients:
    - Lay out the bread slices and cheese slices or shredded cheese.
    - Butter one side of each bread slice with softened butter or margarine.
2. Assemble the sandwiches:
    - Place a slice of cheese or a generous amount of shredded cheese between two bread slices, with the buttered sides facing outwards.
3. Heat the cooking surface:
    - If using a campfire, place a cast-iron skillet or grill pan over the hot coals. If using a camping stove, heat a skillet or griddle over medium heat.
4. Cook the sandwiches:

- Once the skillet or cooking surface is hot, place the assembled sandwiches in the skillet or on the griddle, buttered side down.
- Cook for 2-3 minutes, or until the bottom side of the sandwich is golden brown and crispy.
5. Flip and cook the other side:
    - Carefully flip the sandwiches with a spatula.
    - Continue to cook for another 2-3 minutes, or until the other side is golden brown and crispy, and the cheese is melted.
6. Serve:
    - Once the grilled cheese sandwiches are cooked to your liking, remove them from the skillet or griddle.
    - Cut the sandwiches in half, if desired, and serve immediately while warm and gooey.

Grilled cheese sandwiches are delicious on their own, or you can serve them with a side of soup, salad, or chips for a complete meal. They're quick and easy to make, making them perfect for camping trips, picnics, or anytime you're craving a comforting and satisfying meal.

Fruit Kabobs

Ingredients:

- Assorted fruits (such as strawberries, pineapple chunks, grapes, melon balls, kiwi slices, and berries)
- Wooden or metal skewers

Instructions:

1. Prepare the fruits:
   - Wash and dry all the fruits thoroughly.
   - Prepare the fruits by cutting them into bite-sized pieces, if necessary. Remove stems, seeds, and cores as needed.
2. Assemble the kabobs:
   - Thread the fruit onto the skewers, alternating between different fruits to create a colorful pattern.
   - Leave a little space at the bottom and top of each skewer for easy handling.
3. Serve:
   - Arrange the fruit kabobs on a serving platter or plate.
   - Serve the fruit kabobs immediately, or cover and refrigerate until ready to serve.
4. Optional toppings:
   - You can drizzle the fruit kabobs with honey, maple syrup, or a fruit glaze for added sweetness and flavor.
   - Alternatively, you can serve the fruit kabobs with a side of yogurt or whipped cream for dipping.
5. Enjoy:
   - Fruit kabobs are a delightful and healthy snack or dessert that's perfect for any occasion. Enjoy the fresh and juicy flavors of the fruits with each bite!

Fruit kabobs are highly customizable, so feel free to use your favorite fruits or whatever fruits are in season. Get creative with different combinations and arrangements to make your fruit kabobs visually appealing and delicious. They're a fun and easy way to enjoy the natural sweetness of fresh fruits!

Veggie Skewers

Ingredients:

- Assorted vegetables (such as bell peppers, cherry tomatoes, zucchini, yellow squash, mushrooms, red onion, and eggplant)
- Wooden or metal skewers
- Olive oil
- Salt and pepper
- Optional seasonings (such as garlic powder, Italian seasoning, or balsamic vinegar)

Instructions:

1. Prepare the vegetables:
    - Wash and dry all the vegetables thoroughly.
    - Cut the vegetables into bite-sized pieces, keeping them uniform in size so they cook evenly on the skewers.
2. Pre-soak wooden skewers:
    - If you're using wooden skewers, soak them in water for at least 30 minutes before assembling the veggie skewers. This helps prevent them from burning on the grill.
3. Assemble the skewers:
    - Thread the vegetable pieces onto the skewers, alternating between different vegetables to create a colorful pattern.
    - Leave a little space at the bottom and top of each skewer for easy handling.
4. Season the skewers:
    - Brush the assembled veggie skewers with olive oil to coat them evenly.
    - Season with salt, pepper, and any other desired seasonings, such as garlic powder or Italian seasoning.
5. Grill the skewers:
    - Preheat a grill to medium-high heat.
    - Place the veggie skewers on the grill grate and cook for 8-10 minutes, turning occasionally, until the vegetables are tender and slightly charred.
6. Serve:
    - Once the veggie skewers are cooked to your liking, remove them from the grill.

- Arrange the skewers on a serving platter and serve immediately.
7. Optional garnish:
    - Garnish the veggie skewers with fresh herbs, such as parsley or basil, before serving for added flavor and visual appeal.

Veggie skewers are a healthy and delicious dish that's perfect for vegetarians and meat-lovers alike. They're versatile, easy to customize, and can be served as a side dish or a main course. Enjoy the vibrant colors and flavors of grilled vegetables with every bite!

Campfire Nachos

Ingredients:

- Tortilla chips
- Shredded cheese (such as cheddar, Monterey Jack, or a Mexican blend)
- Cooked protein (such as seasoned ground beef, shredded chicken, or beans)
- Sliced jalapeños
- Diced tomatoes
- Sliced black olives
- Chopped onions
- Guacamole or diced avocado
- Sour cream
- Salsa
- Optional toppings: chopped cilantro, green onions, or hot sauce

Instructions:

1. Prepare the campfire:
    - Build a campfire and let it burn down to hot coals. You'll need a bed of hot coals to cook the nachos.
2. Assemble the nachos:
    - Spread a layer of tortilla chips on the bottom of a cast-iron skillet or disposable aluminum foil tray.
    - Sprinkle a layer of shredded cheese over the tortilla chips.
    - Add a layer of cooked protein (such as seasoned ground beef, shredded chicken, or beans) over the cheese.
    - Sprinkle sliced jalapeños, diced tomatoes, sliced black olives, and chopped onions over the protein layer.
    - Repeat the layers if desired, depending on the size of your skillet or tray.
3. Cook over the campfire:
    - Place the skillet or foil tray directly on the hot coals of the campfire.
    - Cook for about 5-10 minutes, or until the cheese is melted and bubbly, and the nachos are heated through.
4. Serve:
    - Once the nachos are cooked to your liking, carefully remove them from the campfire using heat-resistant gloves or oven mitts.
    - Serve the campfire nachos immediately, while they're hot.

- Top with guacamole or diced avocado, sour cream, salsa, and any other desired toppings.
- Garnish with chopped cilantro, green onions, or hot sauce if desired.

Campfire nachos are a delicious and customizable snack or meal that's perfect for camping trips, backyard cookouts, or any outdoor gathering. Enjoy the cheesy, crunchy goodness of nachos with all your favorite toppings, cooked over the open flame of a campfire!

Pita Pizzas

Ingredients:

- Pita bread rounds (whole wheat or white)
- Pizza sauce
- Shredded mozzarella cheese
- Toppings of your choice (such as pepperoni, sliced bell peppers, onions, mushrooms, olives, cooked sausage, or any other desired toppings)
- Olive oil
- Optional seasonings (such as garlic powder, Italian seasoning, or red pepper flakes)

Instructions:

1. Prepare the ingredients:
    - Lay out the pita bread rounds and prepare your desired pizza toppings.
2. Preheat the grill or campfire:
    - If using a grill, preheat it to medium heat. If cooking over a campfire, make sure you have a bed of hot coals ready.
3. Assemble the pita pizzas:
    - Brush one side of each pita bread round with olive oil.
    - Spread a layer of pizza sauce over the oiled side of each pita bread round.
    - Sprinkle shredded mozzarella cheese over the pizza sauce.
    - Add your desired toppings on top of the cheese.
4. Season the pizzas:
    - Sprinkle optional seasonings, such as garlic powder, Italian seasoning, or red pepper flakes, over the assembled pizzas, if desired.
5. Cook the pizzas:
    - If using a grill, place the assembled pita pizzas directly on the grill grates.
    - If cooking over a campfire, place the pizzas on a grill grate or on a piece of aluminum foil on the hot coals.
    - Cook for about 5-7 minutes, or until the cheese is melted and bubbly, and the edges of the pita bread are crispy.
6. Serve:
    - Once the pizzas are cooked to your liking, carefully remove them from the grill or campfire.

- Transfer the pizzas to a cutting board and let them cool for a minute or two before slicing.
- Slice the pita pizzas into wedges or squares and serve hot.

Pita pizzas are a delicious and customizable meal that's perfect for camping trips, backyard cookouts, or anytime you want a quick and easy dinner option. Enjoy experimenting with different toppings and seasonings to create your perfect pita pizza!

Campfire Sausage and Veggie Foil Packets

Ingredients:

- Sausages (such as pork, chicken, or turkey sausages), sliced
- Assorted vegetables (such as bell peppers, onions, zucchini, yellow squash, mushrooms, and cherry tomatoes), chopped or sliced
- Olive oil or melted butter
- Salt and pepper
- Garlic powder
- Italian seasoning
- Heavy-duty aluminum foil

Instructions:

1. Preheat the grill or campfire:
    - If using a grill, preheat it to medium-high heat. If cooking over a campfire, make sure you have a bed of hot coals ready.
2. Prepare the foil packets:
    - Tear off sheets of heavy-duty aluminum foil, large enough to wrap around the sausage and vegetable mixture.
    - Place a portion of sliced sausages and chopped vegetables in the center of each foil sheet.
3. Season the mixture:
    - Drizzle olive oil or melted butter over the sausage and vegetable mixture.
    - Season with salt, pepper, garlic powder, and Italian seasoning to taste.
    - Toss the mixture gently to coat everything evenly with the seasonings.
4. Wrap the foil packets:
    - Fold the foil over the sausage and vegetable mixture to create a tight packet.
    - Fold the edges of the foil over several times to seal the packet completely, leaving a little room for steam to circulate inside.
5. Cook the foil packets:
    - Place the foil packets directly on the grill grates or on a grate over the campfire.
    - Cook for about 15-20 minutes, turning once halfway through cooking, until the sausages are cooked through and the vegetables are tender.
6. Serve:

- Once the foil packets are cooked to your liking, carefully remove them from the grill or campfire.
- Open the foil packets carefully to avoid steam burns.
- Transfer the sausage and veggie mixture to plates or bowls and serve hot.

Campfire sausage and veggie foil packets are a flavorful and satisfying meal that's easy to customize with your favorite sausage and vegetables. Enjoy the delicious combination of flavors and the convenience of cooking everything together in a foil packet over the open flame of a campfire or grill!

Campfire Corn on the Cob

Ingredients:

- Fresh corn on the cob, still in the husk
- Butter
- Salt
- Aluminum foil

Instructions:

1. Start by preparing your campfire. You'll want to have a good bed of hot coals to cook the corn over.
2. Peel back the husks of the corn, but don't remove them completely. You want to leave them attached at the base.
3. Remove the silk from the corn cob.
4. Rub butter all over the corn cob, then sprinkle with salt to taste.
5. Pull the husks back up over the corn cob, covering it completely.
6. Wrap the corn cob tightly in aluminum foil.
7. Place the wrapped corn directly onto the hot coals of the campfire.
8. Cook for about 15-20 minutes, turning occasionally, until the corn is tender and cooked through.
9. Carefully remove the corn from the fire, unwrap it from the foil, and let it cool slightly before serving.

Enjoy your delicious campfire corn on the cob!

Campfire Hot Dogs

Ingredients:

- Hot dogs
- Hot dog buns
- Condiments of your choice (ketchup, mustard, relish, etc.)

Instructions:

1. Prepare your campfire by building a good bed of hot coals.
2. Thread a skewer or long stick through each hot dog. Make sure the hot dog is securely attached to the skewer.
3. Hold the hot dog over the campfire, rotating it occasionally to ensure even cooking.
4. Cook the hot dog until it's heated through and has some char marks on the outside. This usually takes about 5-7 minutes, depending on the heat of your fire.
5. Carefully remove the hot dog from the skewer and place it in a bun.
6. Add your favorite condiments to the hot dog.
7. Enjoy your delicious campfire hot dog!

You can get creative with your toppings and even roast some marshmallows for dessert while you're at it.

Campfire Baked Beans

Ingredients:

- 2 cans (15 oz each) of baked beans
- ½ cup barbecue sauce
- 2 tablespoons brown sugar
- 2 slices bacon, chopped
- ¼ cup diced onion
- Salt and pepper to taste

Instructions:

1. Start by preparing your campfire. You'll want to have a good bed of hot coals to cook your beans over.
2. In a cast iron skillet or a sturdy aluminum foil packet, combine the baked beans, barbecue sauce, brown sugar, chopped bacon, diced onion, salt, and pepper.
3. Mix everything together well.
4. Place the skillet or foil packet directly onto the hot coals of the campfire.
5. Cook the beans for about 15-20 minutes, stirring occasionally, until they are heated through and bubbling.
6. Carefully remove the skillet or foil packet from the fire using heat-resistant gloves or tongs.
7. Let the beans cool slightly before serving.

Enjoy your delicious campfire baked beans as a side dish to your outdoor meal!

Grilled Pineapple Slices

Ingredients:

- Fresh pineapple
- Olive oil or melted butter (optional)
- Honey or brown sugar (optional)
- Cinnamon (optional)
- Mint leaves for garnish (optional)

Instructions:

1. Preheat your grill or campfire grate to medium-high heat.
2. Peel the pineapple and remove the core.
3. Cut the pineapple into slices, about 1/2 to 3/4 inch thick.
4. If desired, lightly brush both sides of the pineapple slices with olive oil or melted butter. This helps prevent sticking and adds flavor.
5. Optionally, sprinkle some honey or brown sugar over the pineapple slices for added sweetness. You can also sprinkle a pinch of cinnamon for extra flavor.
6. Place the pineapple slices directly onto the grill or campfire grate.
7. Grill the pineapple slices for about 3-5 minutes on each side, or until they develop grill marks and start to caramelize.
8. Carefully remove the grilled pineapple slices from the grill and transfer them to a serving platter.
9. Garnish with fresh mint leaves if desired.
10. Serve the grilled pineapple slices hot as a side dish or dessert.

Enjoy the delicious combination of smoky, caramelized flavor and natural sweetness in these grilled pineapple slices!

Grilled Peach Halves

Ingredients:

- Fresh peaches
- Olive oil or melted butter
- Honey (optional)
- Cinnamon (optional)
- Vanilla ice cream (optional, for serving)

Instructions:

1. Preheat your grill or campfire grate to medium heat.
2. Cut the peaches in half and remove the pits.
3. Lightly brush the cut side of each peach half with olive oil or melted butter. This helps prevent sticking and adds flavor.
4. Optionally, drizzle honey over the cut side of each peach half for added sweetness. You can also sprinkle a pinch of cinnamon for extra flavor.
5. Place the peach halves cut-side down on the grill or campfire grate.
6. Grill the peach halves for about 3-4 minutes on each side, or until they develop grill marks and start to caramelize.
7. Carefully remove the grilled peach halves from the grill and transfer them to a serving platter.
8. Serve the grilled peach halves warm as a side dish, dessert, or a topping for vanilla ice cream.

Grilled peach halves are delicious on their own or paired with ice cream for a decadent summer treat. Enjoy!

Grilled Watermelon Slices

Ingredients:

- Watermelon slices (about 1-inch thick)
- Olive oil or melted butter
- Honey or maple syrup (optional)
- Lime juice (optional)
- Sea salt or chili powder (optional)
- Fresh mint leaves for garnish (optional)

Instructions:

1. Preheat your grill or campfire grate to medium-high heat.
2. Cut the watermelon into slices, about 1 inch thick, and remove the rind.
3. Lightly brush both sides of each watermelon slice with olive oil or melted butter. This helps prevent sticking and adds flavor.
4. Optionally, drizzle honey or maple syrup over the watermelon slices for added sweetness. You can also squeeze some fresh lime juice over them for a tangy flavor.
5. If you like a sweet and savory combination, sprinkle a pinch of sea salt or chili powder over the watermelon slices.
6. Place the watermelon slices directly onto the grill or campfire grate.
7. Grill the watermelon slices for about 2-3 minutes on each side, or until they develop grill marks and start to caramelize slightly.
8. Carefully remove the grilled watermelon slices from the grill and transfer them to a serving platter.
9. Garnish with fresh mint leaves if desired.
10. Serve the grilled watermelon slices warm as a unique and refreshing appetizer or side dish.

Grilled watermelon slices are a delightful combination of smoky, caramelized flavor and juicy sweetness. Enjoy this creative summer treat!

Foil Packet Fish

Ingredients:

- Fish fillets (such as salmon, tilapia, trout, or any firm white fish)
- Lemon slices
- Fresh herbs (such as dill, parsley, or thyme)
- Olive oil or melted butter
- Salt and pepper to taste
- Optional: minced garlic, thinly sliced onions, cherry tomatoes, or any other desired vegetables or seasonings

Instructions:

1. Preheat your oven to 400°F (200°C) or prepare your grill or campfire for cooking.
2. Tear off a large piece of aluminum foil for each fish fillet, making sure it's big enough to wrap the fish completely.
3. Place each fish fillet in the center of a piece of foil. Season both sides of the fish with salt and pepper.
4. Drizzle some olive oil or melted butter over each fish fillet.
5. Place a couple of lemon slices and some fresh herbs on top of each fish fillet. You can also add any optional vegetables or seasonings at this point.
6. Fold the sides of the foil over the fish to create a packet, making sure it's sealed tightly to prevent any juices from leaking out.
7. If using an oven, place the foil packets on a baking sheet and bake for about 15-20 minutes, depending on the thickness of the fish fillets. If using a grill or campfire, place the foil packets directly on the grill grate or coals and cook for a similar amount of time, flipping halfway through.
8. Carefully open the foil packets (watch out for steam) and check if the fish is cooked through and flakes easily with a fork. If not, reseal the packets and continue cooking for a few more minutes.
9. Once the fish is cooked to your liking, carefully transfer the foil packets to serving plates.
10. Serve the foil packet fish immediately, either directly in the foil packets or transferred to plates, and enjoy!

Foil packet fish is not only easy to make but also results in tender, flavorful fish with minimal cleanup. Feel free to customize the seasonings and add your favorite vegetables to make it your own!

Campfire Chicken Fajitas

Ingredients:

- 1 pound boneless, skinless chicken breasts, thinly sliced
- 2 bell peppers (any color), thinly sliced
- 1 onion, thinly sliced
- 2 cloves garlic, minced
- 2 tablespoons olive oil
- 2 tablespoons fajita seasoning (store-bought or homemade)
- Salt and pepper to taste
- Flour tortillas
- Optional toppings: shredded cheese, salsa, sour cream, guacamole, chopped cilantro, lime wedges

Instructions:

1. Start by preparing your campfire. You'll want to have a good bed of hot coals to cook your fajitas over.
2. In a large bowl, combine the sliced chicken, bell peppers, onion, minced garlic, olive oil, and fajita seasoning. Toss until everything is evenly coated. Season with salt and pepper to taste.
3. Tear off several large sheets of heavy-duty aluminum foil, each large enough to wrap a portion of the fajita mixture.
4. Divide the chicken and vegetable mixture evenly among the foil sheets, placing it in the center of each sheet.
5. Fold the sides of each foil sheet over the chicken and vegetable mixture, then fold up the ends to seal the packets tightly.
6. Place the foil packets directly onto the hot coals of the campfire.
7. Cook the foil packets for about 15-20 minutes, flipping them halfway through, until the chicken is cooked through and the vegetables are tender.
8. Carefully remove the foil packets from the fire using heat-resistant gloves or tongs.
9. Open the foil packets carefully (watch out for steam) and check that the chicken is fully cooked.
10. Warm the flour tortillas over the campfire or on a grill grate for a minute or two on each side.
11. Serve the chicken fajita mixture in the warm tortillas, along with your choice of toppings.

12. Enjoy your delicious campfire chicken fajitas with all the fixings!

This recipe is versatile, so feel free to customize it with your favorite vegetables or additional seasonings to suit your taste.

Campfire Meatball Subs

Ingredients:

- 1 pound ground beef or turkey
- 1/2 cup breadcrumbs
- 1/4 cup grated Parmesan cheese
- 1 egg
- 1/4 cup chopped fresh parsley (optional)
- Salt and pepper to taste
- Olive oil
- Marinara sauce
- Sub rolls
- Sliced mozzarella cheese
- Optional toppings: sliced onions, bell peppers, mushrooms

Instructions:

1. Start by preparing your campfire. You'll want to have a good bed of hot coals to cook your meatballs over.
2. In a large bowl, combine the ground beef or turkey, breadcrumbs, Parmesan cheese, egg, chopped parsley (if using), salt, and pepper. Mix until well combined.
3. Roll the meat mixture into small meatballs, about 1 inch in diameter.
4. Heat a cast iron skillet over the campfire or on a grill grate. Drizzle some olive oil in the skillet.
5. Place the meatballs in the skillet and cook, turning occasionally, until browned on all sides and cooked through, about 10-15 minutes.
6. Once the meatballs are cooked, pour marinara sauce over them in the skillet and stir to coat.
7. Split the sub rolls lengthwise, but not all the way through.
8. Place a few meatballs and some sauce in each sub roll.
9. Top the meatballs with sliced mozzarella cheese.
10. If desired, add any optional toppings like sliced onions, bell peppers, or mushrooms.
11. Wrap each sub in aluminum foil, sealing it tightly.
12. Place the foil-wrapped subs on the hot coals of the campfire and cook for about 5-10 minutes, or until the cheese is melted and the subs are heated through.

13. Carefully remove the foil-wrapped subs from the fire using heat-resistant gloves or tongs.
14. Unwrap the foil and serve the meatball subs hot.

Enjoy your delicious campfire meatball subs! They're perfect for a satisfying outdoor meal.

Campfire Chili

Ingredients:

- 1 pound ground beef
- 1 onion, chopped
- 2 cloves garlic, minced
- 1 bell pepper, chopped
- 1 can (15 oz) kidney beans, drained and rinsed
- 1 can (15 oz) black beans, drained and rinsed
- 1 can (15 oz) diced tomatoes
- 1 can (6 oz) tomato paste
- 2 cups beef broth or water
- 2 tablespoons chili powder
- 1 tablespoon cumin
- 1 teaspoon paprika
- Salt and pepper to taste
- Optional toppings: shredded cheese, sour cream, chopped green onions, diced avocado, cilantro, tortilla chips

Instructions:

1. Start by preparing your campfire. You'll want to have a sturdy cooking pot or Dutch oven and a good bed of hot coals to cook your chili over.
2. Heat the cooking pot over the campfire and add the ground beef. Cook, breaking it apart with a spoon, until browned.
3. Add the chopped onion, minced garlic, and chopped bell pepper to the pot. Cook until the vegetables are softened, about 5 minutes.
4. Stir in the kidney beans, black beans, diced tomatoes, tomato paste, beef broth or water, chili powder, cumin, paprika, salt, and pepper.
5. Bring the chili to a simmer, then reduce the heat and let it cook over the campfire for about 30-40 minutes, stirring occasionally, until the flavors have melded together and the chili has thickened to your desired consistency.
6. Taste and adjust the seasoning if necessary.
7. Once the chili is ready, remove it from the heat and let it cool slightly before serving.
8. Ladle the chili into bowls and top with your favorite toppings, such as shredded cheese, sour cream, chopped green onions, diced avocado, cilantro, or crushed tortilla chips.

9. Serve the campfire chili hot and enjoy!

This hearty chili is sure to warm you up and satisfy your hunger after a day spent outdoors. Plus, it's easy to customize with your favorite ingredients and toppings.

Campfire Mac and Cheese

Ingredients:

- 8 oz elbow macaroni or any pasta of your choice
- 2 cups shredded cheddar cheese (or a mix of your favorite cheeses)
- 2 tablespoons butter
- 2 tablespoons all-purpose flour
- 2 cups milk
- Salt and pepper to taste
- Optional toppings: breadcrumbs, chopped bacon, diced tomatoes, chopped parsley

Instructions:

1. Start by preparing your campfire. You'll need a sturdy cooking pot or Dutch oven and a good bed of hot coals to cook your mac and cheese over.
2. Cook the pasta according to the package instructions until al dente. Drain and set aside.
3. In the cooking pot or Dutch oven, melt the butter over the campfire.
4. Stir in the flour and cook for 1-2 minutes, until lightly golden and fragrant.
5. Slowly pour in the milk, stirring constantly to prevent lumps from forming.
6. Cook the mixture, stirring frequently, until it thickens enough to coat the back of a spoon, about 5-7 minutes.
7. Stir in the shredded cheese until melted and smooth.
8. Add the cooked pasta to the cheese sauce and stir to combine.
9. Season the mac and cheese with salt and pepper to taste.
10. If desired, sprinkle breadcrumbs over the top of the mac and cheese for a crunchy topping.
11. Cover the pot or Dutch oven and let the mac and cheese cook over the campfire for about 5-10 minutes, until heated through and bubbly.
12. Remove the pot or Dutch oven from the heat and let the mac and cheese cool slightly before serving.
13. Garnish with optional toppings such as chopped bacon, diced tomatoes, or chopped parsley if desired.
14. Serve the campfire mac and cheese hot and enjoy the creamy, cheesy goodness!

This simple and satisfying dish is sure to be a hit with everyone around the campfire.

Feel free to customize it with your favorite cheeses or add-ins to make it your own.

Campfire Breakfast Burritos

Ingredients:

- 6 large eggs
- 1 tablespoon butter or oil
- Salt and pepper to taste
- 6 large flour tortillas
- 1 cup shredded cheese (cheddar, Monterey Jack, or your favorite)
- 1 cup cooked breakfast sausage, bacon, or ham, diced
- Optional toppings: salsa, diced tomatoes, sliced avocado, sour cream, chopped cilantro

Instructions:

1. Start by preparing your campfire. You'll need a skillet or griddle and a good bed of hot coals to cook your breakfast burritos over.
2. In a bowl, whisk the eggs until well beaten. Season with salt and pepper to taste.
3. Heat the butter or oil in the skillet over the campfire.
4. Pour the beaten eggs into the skillet and cook, stirring occasionally, until scrambled and cooked through.
5. Remove the skillet from the heat and set aside.
6. Lay out the flour tortillas on a clean surface.
7. Divide the scrambled eggs evenly among the tortillas, spreading them out in a line down the center of each tortilla.
8. Sprinkle shredded cheese over the scrambled eggs on each tortilla.
9. Add a portion of cooked breakfast sausage, bacon, or ham on top of the cheese on each tortilla.
10. If desired, add any optional toppings such as salsa, diced tomatoes, sliced avocado, sour cream, or chopped cilantro.
11. Fold the sides of each tortilla over the filling, then roll it up tightly to form a burrito.
12. Wrap each burrito in aluminum foil, sealing it tightly.
13. Place the foil-wrapped breakfast burritos on the hot coals of the campfire and cook for about 5-10 minutes, turning occasionally, until heated through.
14. Carefully remove the foil-wrapped burritos from the fire using heat-resistant gloves or tongs.
15. Unwrap the foil and serve the breakfast burritos hot.

16. Enjoy your delicious campfire breakfast burritos, packed with eggs, cheese, and your favorite breakfast meats and toppings!

These breakfast burritos are portable, customizable, and perfect for fueling up before a day of outdoor adventures. Feel free to customize them with your favorite ingredients to make them your own!

Pancake Skewers

Ingredients:

- Pancake batter (homemade or store-bought)
- Your choice of pancake toppings (such as chocolate chips, blueberries, strawberries, bananas, nuts, or mini marshmallows)
- Wooden skewers

Instructions:

1. Prepare your pancake batter according to your favorite recipe or package instructions. Make sure it's thick enough to hold its shape on the skewers.
2. Preheat a griddle or non-stick skillet over medium heat.
3. Thread your desired toppings onto wooden skewers, leaving a little space at the top for flipping.
4. Pour small amounts of pancake batter onto the griddle or skillet, forming small circles about the same size as your skewers.
5. Immediately place a skewer with toppings onto each pancake circle, pressing it down slightly so the toppings sink into the batter.
6. Cook the pancakes for a few minutes on one side until bubbles form on the surface, then carefully flip them using a spatula.
7. Cook for another minute or two on the other side until golden brown and cooked through.
8. Once the pancake skewers are cooked, remove them from the griddle or skillet and let them cool slightly before serving.
9. Serve the pancake skewers warm with your favorite toppings such as maple syrup, whipped cream, or additional fresh fruit.
10. Enjoy your delicious and fun pancake skewers for breakfast or brunch!

These pancake skewers are sure to be a hit with kids and adults alike. They're easy to customize with your favorite pancake toppings and are perfect for enjoying on the go.

Grilled Peanut Butter and Jelly Sandwiches

Ingredients:

- Bread (white, whole wheat, or your preferred variety)
- Peanut butter
- Jelly or jam of your choice
- Butter or margarine, softened

Instructions:

1. Spread peanut butter on one slice of bread and jelly or jam on another slice, ensuring even coverage to the edges.
2. Place the two slices of bread together to form a sandwich, with the peanut butter and jelly sides facing each other.
3. Lightly spread butter or margarine on the outer sides of the sandwich. This will help the bread toast evenly and develop a golden crust.
4. Preheat a skillet or griddle over medium heat.
5. Carefully place the sandwich onto the skillet or griddle, buttered side down.
6. Cook the sandwich for 2-3 minutes on each side, or until the bread is golden brown and crispy, and the peanut butter and jelly are warm and melty.
7. Use a spatula to carefully flip the sandwich and cook the other side until it's golden brown and crispy as well.
8. Once both sides are grilled to perfection, remove the sandwich from the skillet or griddle.
9. Allow the sandwich to cool for a moment before slicing it diagonally or into halves.
10. Serve your grilled peanut butter and jelly sandwiches warm and enjoy the comforting, nostalgic flavors!

These sandwiches are a delightful treat for breakfast, lunch, or even a cozy snack. Feel free to experiment with different types of bread, nut butters, and jelly or jam flavors to suit your taste preferences.

Campfire Stuffed Peppers

Ingredients:

- Bell peppers (any color), halved and seeds removed
- 1 pound ground beef or turkey
- 1 small onion, chopped
- 2 cloves garlic, minced
- 1 cup cooked rice (white or brown)
- 1 can (14.5 oz) diced tomatoes, drained
- 1 cup shredded cheese (cheddar, mozzarella, or your favorite)
- Salt and pepper to taste
- Optional toppings: chopped fresh parsley, sliced green onions, sour cream

Instructions:

1. Prepare your campfire. You'll need a sturdy cooking grate or a grill with hot coals.
2. In a large skillet, cook the ground beef or turkey over the campfire until browned, breaking it apart with a spoon as it cooks.
3. Add the chopped onion and minced garlic to the skillet and cook until the onion is soft and translucent, about 5 minutes.
4. Stir in the cooked rice and diced tomatoes, and season with salt and pepper to taste. Cook for an additional 2-3 minutes to allow the flavors to meld together.
5. Remove the skillet from the heat and stir in half of the shredded cheese until melted and combined.
6. Stuff each halved bell pepper with the meat and rice mixture, pressing it down slightly to fill the peppers evenly.
7. Sprinkle the remaining shredded cheese over the tops of the stuffed peppers.
8. Place the stuffed peppers on the cooking grate or grill over the campfire.
9. Cover the peppers with aluminum foil and let them cook for about 15-20 minutes, or until the peppers are tender and the cheese is melted and bubbly.
10. Carefully remove the stuffed peppers from the campfire using heat-resistant gloves or tongs.
11. Garnish the stuffed peppers with chopped fresh parsley, sliced green onions, or a dollop of sour cream if desired.
12. Serve the campfire stuffed peppers hot and enjoy the delicious and flavorful meal!

These stuffed peppers are versatile and can be customized with your favorite ingredients. Feel free to add diced vegetables, beans, or different types of cheese to make them your own.

Campfire Chicken Wings

Ingredients:

- Chicken wings
- BBQ sauce or marinade of your choice
- Salt and pepper to taste
- Optional: additional spices or herbs for seasoning

Instructions:

1. Start by preparing your campfire. You'll need a grill grate or cooking grate positioned over hot coals.
2. Season the chicken wings with salt, pepper, and any additional spices or herbs you like. You can use a premade seasoning blend or create your own.
3. If using BBQ sauce or marinade, you can either brush it onto the chicken wings now or wait until they're partially cooked on the grill.
4. Place the seasoned chicken wings on the grill grate over the campfire.
5. Cook the chicken wings for about 15-20 minutes, turning occasionally, until they're cooked through and have a nice charred exterior.
6. If you haven't already applied BBQ sauce or marinade, brush it onto the chicken wings during the last few minutes of cooking, allowing it to caramelize and infuse the wings with flavor.
7. Once the chicken wings are cooked to your liking and have a deliciously charred exterior, remove them from the grill grate and transfer them to a serving platter.
8. Serve the campfire chicken wings hot, along with your favorite dipping sauces or sides.

These campfire chicken wings are sure to be a hit at your outdoor gathering. They're perfect for enjoying with friends and family while soaking in the beauty of nature. Feel free to adjust the seasonings and sauces to suit your taste preferences!

Campfire Sausage and Potato Hash

Ingredients:

- 1 pound sausage (such as breakfast sausage or smoked sausage), sliced
- 4 large potatoes, diced
- 1 onion, chopped
- 1 bell pepper, chopped
- 2 cloves garlic, minced
- 2 tablespoons olive oil
- Salt and pepper to taste
- Optional seasonings: paprika, thyme, rosemary, or any herbs and spices you like
- Optional toppings: chopped parsley, green onions, shredded cheese, hot sauce

Instructions:

1. Start by preparing your campfire. You'll want to have a sturdy cooking grate positioned over hot coals.
2. In a large cast iron skillet or Dutch oven, heat the olive oil over the campfire.
3. Add the sliced sausage to the skillet and cook until browned and cooked through, stirring occasionally.
4. Once the sausage is cooked, add the diced potatoes, chopped onion, chopped bell pepper, and minced garlic to the skillet.
5. Season the mixture with salt, pepper, and any optional seasonings you like. Stir to combine everything well.
6. Cook the sausage and potato mixture over the campfire, stirring occasionally, until the potatoes are tender and browned, and the onions and peppers are softened.
7. Depending on the heat of your fire, this could take about 20-30 minutes.
8. Once the sausage and potato hash is cooked to your liking, remove the skillet from the campfire.
9. Sprinkle optional toppings such as chopped parsley, green onions, shredded cheese, or hot sauce over the hash before serving.
10. Serve the campfire sausage and potato hash hot, either as a main dish or as a side dish alongside eggs for breakfast or grilled meat for dinner.

This hearty and flavorful dish is sure to be a hit with everyone around the campfire. Feel free to customize it with your favorite ingredients and seasonings!

Campfire Breakfast Hash

Ingredients:

- 1 pound potatoes, diced
- 1 onion, diced
- 1 bell pepper, diced
- 8 ounces breakfast sausage or bacon, diced
- 4 large eggs
- Salt and pepper to taste
- Optional toppings: shredded cheese, chopped green onions, hot sauce

Instructions:

1. Start by preparing your campfire. You'll want to have a sturdy cooking grate positioned over hot coals.
2. Heat a large cast iron skillet or Dutch oven over the campfire.
3. Add the diced potatoes to the skillet and cook, stirring occasionally, until they start to brown and become tender, about 10 minutes.
4. Add the diced onion, bell pepper, and breakfast sausage or bacon to the skillet. Cook, stirring occasionally, until the vegetables are softened and the sausage or bacon is cooked through, about 5-7 minutes.
5. Create four wells in the hash mixture with a spoon. Crack one egg into each well.
6. Season the hash with salt and pepper to taste.
7. Cover the skillet with a lid or foil and let the eggs cook until the whites are set and the yolks reach your desired level of doneness, about 5-7 minutes for runny yolks or longer for firmer yolks.
8. Once the eggs are cooked to your liking, remove the skillet from the campfire.
9. Sprinkle optional toppings such as shredded cheese, chopped green onions, or hot sauce over the hash before serving.
10. Serve the campfire breakfast hash hot, directly from the skillet, and enjoy a delicious and hearty start to your day in the great outdoors!

This versatile dish can be customized with your favorite ingredients and toppings, so feel free to get creative and make it your own. Whether you're camping, hiking, or just enjoying a leisurely morning in nature, campfire breakfast hash is sure to be a hit!

Campfire French Toast

Ingredients:

- 8 slices of bread (white, whole wheat, or your favorite type)
- 4 large eggs
- 1/2 cup milk (or substitute with half-and-half or heavy cream for richer French toast)
- 1 teaspoon vanilla extract
- 1/2 teaspoon ground cinnamon
- Butter or oil for greasing the cooking surface
- Maple syrup, powdered sugar, or your favorite toppings for serving

Instructions:

1. Start by preparing your campfire. You'll need a sturdy cooking grate or skillet positioned over hot coals.
2. In a shallow dish or bowl, whisk together the eggs, milk, vanilla extract, and ground cinnamon until well combined.
3. Dip each slice of bread into the egg mixture, ensuring that both sides are coated evenly.
4. Heat a skillet or griddle over the campfire and grease it with butter or oil to prevent sticking.
5. Place the coated bread slices onto the skillet or griddle and cook for 2-3 minutes on each side, or until golden brown and cooked through.
6. Depending on the size of your cooking surface, you may need to cook the French toast in batches.
7. Once cooked, transfer the French toast to a serving platter.
8. Serve the campfire French toast hot, topped with maple syrup, powdered sugar, or your favorite toppings.
9. Enjoy the delicious and comforting flavors of campfire French toast as a perfect start to your outdoor adventure or leisurely morning in nature!

Feel free to customize your campfire French toast by adding additional toppings such as fresh berries, sliced bananas, chopped nuts, or whipped cream. It's a versatile dish that's sure to be a hit with everyone around the campfire!

Campfire Cereal Bars

Ingredients:

- 4 cups crispy rice cereal (such as Rice Krispies)
- 1/2 cup peanut butter or almond butter
- 1/2 cup honey or maple syrup
- 1 teaspoon vanilla extract
- 1/2 cup chocolate chips or chopped nuts (optional)

Instructions:

1. Start by preparing your campfire. You won't need direct heat for this recipe, so you can either cook indoors or prepare a cooking area away from the flames.
2. In a large mixing bowl, combine the crispy rice cereal with the chocolate chips or chopped nuts, if using. Set aside.
3. In a small saucepan, heat the peanut butter and honey (or maple syrup) over low heat, stirring constantly, until melted and smooth.
4. Remove the saucepan from the heat and stir in the vanilla extract.
5. Pour the peanut butter mixture over the crispy rice cereal mixture in the mixing bowl.
6. Use a spatula or wooden spoon to gently fold the ingredients together until the cereal is evenly coated with the peanut butter mixture.
7. Line a baking dish or pan with parchment paper, leaving some overhang on the sides for easy removal.
8. Transfer the cereal mixture into the prepared baking dish and press it down firmly and evenly using the back of a spoon or your hands.
9. Place the baking dish in the refrigerator or let it sit at room temperature for at least 1-2 hours, or until the cereal bars are firm and set.
10. Once the cereal bars are firm, use the parchment paper overhang to lift them out of the baking dish.
11. Use a sharp knife to cut the cereal bars into squares or rectangles.
12. Serve the campfire cereal bars as a delicious and portable snack for your outdoor adventures!

These cereal bars are customizable, so feel free to experiment with different add-ins such as dried fruit, seeds, or spices to suit your taste preferences. Store any leftovers in an airtight container for later enjoyment.

Campfire Banana Splits

Ingredients:

- Bananas, ripe but firm
- Chocolate chips
- Mini marshmallows
- Chopped nuts (such as peanuts, almonds, or walnuts)
- Aluminum foil

Optional toppings:

- Whipped cream
- Chocolate syrup
- Caramel sauce
- Maraschino cherries
- Sprinkles

Instructions:

1. Prepare your campfire. You'll want to have a bed of hot coals for cooking.
2. While the fire is heating up, prepare the bananas. Leaving the peel on, slice each banana in half lengthwise, cutting through the peel and just into the banana flesh.
3. Gently pry open the banana halves, creating a space for the toppings.
4. Place the banana halves on a sheet of aluminum foil, making sure they're stable and won't tip over.
5. Fill the banana halves with chocolate chips, mini marshmallows, and chopped nuts. You can use as much or as little of each topping as you like, depending on your preference.
6. Wrap the banana halves tightly in the aluminum foil, sealing them completely.
7. Place the foil-wrapped banana splits on the hot coals of the campfire and cook for about 5-7 minutes, or until the toppings are melted and gooey, and the bananas are soft and caramelized.
8. Carefully remove the foil-wrapped banana splits from the fire using heat-resistant gloves or tongs.
9. Unwrap the foil and transfer the banana splits to serving plates.
10. If desired, top each banana split with whipped cream, chocolate syrup, caramel sauce, maraschino cherries, or sprinkles.

11. Serve the campfire banana splits immediately and enjoy the gooey, chocolatey goodness!

These campfire banana splits are sure to be a hit with kids and adults alike. Feel free to get creative with the toppings and customize them to suit your taste preferences.

Campfire Cobbler

Ingredients:

- 4 cups of your favorite fruit (such as peaches, berries, or apples), sliced or chopped
- 1/2 cup granulated sugar (adjust according to the sweetness of your fruit)
- 1 tablespoon cornstarch (if using fresh fruit) or 2 tablespoons all-purpose flour (if using canned fruit)
- 1 teaspoon ground cinnamon (optional)
- 1 cup all-purpose flour
- 1/2 cup granulated sugar
- 1 teaspoon baking powder
- 1/4 teaspoon salt
- 1/2 cup unsalted butter, melted
- 1/2 cup milk
- Vanilla ice cream or whipped cream for serving (optional)

Instructions:

1. Start by preparing your campfire. You'll want to have a bed of hot coals for cooking.
2. In a bowl, combine the sliced or chopped fruit with granulated sugar, cornstarch (or flour), and ground cinnamon, if using. Toss until the fruit is evenly coated.
3. Transfer the fruit mixture to a cast iron skillet or Dutch oven.
4. In another bowl, whisk together the all-purpose flour, granulated sugar, baking powder, and salt.
5. Stir in the melted butter and milk until just combined, being careful not to overmix.
6. Spoon the batter over the fruit mixture in the skillet or Dutch oven, spreading it out evenly.
7. Cover the skillet or Dutch oven with a lid or aluminum foil.
8. Place the skillet or Dutch oven on the hot coals of the campfire and cook for about 25-35 minutes, or until the cobbler is bubbly and the topping is golden brown and cooked through.
9. Carefully remove the skillet or Dutch oven from the fire using heat-resistant gloves or oven mitts.
10. Let the campfire cobbler cool for a few minutes before serving.

11. Serve the campfire cobbler warm, either on its own or topped with vanilla ice cream or whipped cream for an extra treat.
12. Enjoy the delicious and comforting flavors of campfire cobbler as a perfect ending to your outdoor meal!

Feel free to customize your campfire cobbler by using your favorite fruit and adjusting the sweetness level to suit your taste preferences. It's a versatile dessert that's sure to be a hit around the campfire!

Campfire Rice Krispie Treats

Ingredients:

- 6 cups Rice Krispies cereal
- 1/4 cup unsalted butter
- 1 package (10 oz) marshmallows
- Cooking spray or extra butter for greasing

Instructions:

1. Prepare your campfire. You'll want to have a bed of hot coals for cooking.
2. Grease a large heatproof dish or pan with cooking spray or butter. You can use a disposable aluminum baking dish or a sturdy heatproof container.
3. In a large pot or Dutch oven, melt the butter over the campfire.
4. Add the marshmallows to the pot and stir until they are completely melted and smooth.
5. Remove the pot from the heat and stir in the Rice Krispies cereal until it is evenly coated with the marshmallow mixture.
6. Quickly transfer the mixture to the greased dish or pan.
7. Use a buttered spatula or your hands (sprayed with cooking spray or butter to prevent sticking) to press the mixture firmly and evenly into the dish or pan.
8. Let the Rice Krispie treats cool and set for about 30 minutes to 1 hour.
9. Once the treats are set, cut them into squares or bars using a sharp knife.
10. Serve the campfire Rice Krispie treats and enjoy the gooey, marshmallowy goodness!

These campfire Rice Krispie treats are sure to be a hit with kids and adults alike. They're perfect for enjoying as a sweet treat while sitting around the campfire or for packing as a snack on your outdoor adventures. Feel free to get creative and add in extras like chocolate chips, dried fruit, or nuts for added flavor and texture.

Campfire Apple Crisp

Ingredients:

- 6 cups of apples, peeled, cored, and sliced (such as Granny Smith, Honeycrisp, or Fuji)
- 1/2 cup granulated sugar
- 1 tablespoon lemon juice
- 1 teaspoon ground cinnamon
- 1/4 teaspoon ground nutmeg (optional)
- 1 cup old-fashioned rolled oats
- 1/2 cup all-purpose flour
- 1/2 cup packed brown sugar
- 1/2 cup unsalted butter, melted
- Pinch of salt

Instructions:

1. Start by preparing your campfire. You'll want to have a bed of hot coals for cooking.
2. In a large bowl, combine the sliced apples with granulated sugar, lemon juice, ground cinnamon, and ground nutmeg (if using). Toss until the apples are evenly coated.
3. Transfer the apple mixture to a cast iron skillet or Dutch oven.
4. In another bowl, combine the rolled oats, all-purpose flour, brown sugar, melted butter, and a pinch of salt. Mix until the ingredients are well combined and crumbly.
5. Sprinkle the oat mixture evenly over the top of the apple mixture in the skillet or Dutch oven.
6. Cover the skillet or Dutch oven with a lid or aluminum foil.
7. Place the skillet or Dutch oven on the hot coals of the campfire and cook for about 25-35 minutes, or until the apples are tender and bubbly, and the topping is golden brown and crispy.
8. Carefully remove the skillet or Dutch oven from the fire using heat-resistant gloves or oven mitts.
9. Let the campfire apple crisp cool for a few minutes before serving.
10. Serve the apple crisp warm, either on its own or topped with vanilla ice cream or whipped cream for an extra treat.

11. Enjoy the delicious and comforting flavors of campfire apple crisp as a perfect ending to your outdoor meal!

Feel free to customize your campfire apple crisp by adding extras like chopped nuts or dried fruit to the topping, or by adjusting the sweetness level to suit your taste preferences. It's a versatile dessert that's sure to be a hit around the campfire!Campfire

Peach Melba

Ingredients:

- 4 ripe peaches
- 1/4 cup granulated sugar
- 1/4 cup water
- 1 cup fresh or frozen raspberries
- 2 tablespoons granulated sugar
- Vanilla ice cream
- Fresh mint leaves for garnish (optional)

Instructions:

1. Start by preparing your campfire. You'll want to have a bed of hot coals for cooking.
2. Peel the peaches and cut them in half, removing the pits.
3. In a small saucepan, combine the water and 1/4 cup granulated sugar. Heat the mixture over the campfire, stirring occasionally, until the sugar is dissolved and the syrup is slightly thickened, about 5 minutes.
4. Add the peach halves to the syrup in the saucepan, cut side down. Cook the peaches for about 5-7 minutes, or until they are tender and caramelized, turning them once halfway through cooking.
5. While the peaches are cooking, prepare the raspberry sauce. In another small saucepan, combine the raspberries and 2 tablespoons granulated sugar. Heat the mixture over the campfire, stirring occasionally, until the raspberries break down

and form a sauce, about 5 minutes. Remove the saucepan from the heat and set aside.
6. Once the peaches are cooked, remove them from the saucepan and let them cool slightly.
7. To serve, place a scoop of vanilla ice cream in each serving dish. Top with a caramelized peach half.
8. Spoon the raspberry sauce over the peaches and ice cream.
9. Garnish with fresh mint leaves, if desired.
10. Serve the Campfire Peach Melba immediately and enjoy the delicious combination of flavors and textures!

This Campfire Peach Melba is a delightful and elegant dessert that's perfect for enjoying outdoors. It's a refreshing treat that's sure to impress your guests!

Campfire Bread Pudding

Ingredients:

- 6 cups cubed bread (such as French bread, brioche, or challah)
- 4 large eggs
- 1 1/2 cups milk
- 1/2 cup heavy cream
- 1/2 cup granulated sugar
- 1 teaspoon vanilla extract
- 1/2 teaspoon ground cinnamon
- Pinch of salt
- 1/2 cup raisins or chopped nuts (optional)
- Butter for greasing the baking dish

Instructions:

1. Start by preparing your campfire. You'll want to have a bed of hot coals for cooking.
2. Grease a heatproof dish or pan with butter. You can use a disposable aluminum baking dish or a sturdy heatproof container.
3. Place the cubed bread in the greased dish, spreading it out evenly.
4. In a large bowl, whisk together the eggs, milk, heavy cream, granulated sugar, vanilla extract, ground cinnamon, and a pinch of salt until well combined.
5. Pour the egg mixture over the bread cubes in the dish, making sure all the bread is coated. Press down gently on the bread to help it soak up the liquid.
6. If using raisins or nuts, sprinkle them evenly over the bread mixture.
7. Cover the dish with aluminum foil.
8. Place the dish on the hot coals of the campfire and cook for about 30-40 minutes, or until the bread pudding is set and golden brown on top.
9. Check the bread pudding occasionally to ensure it's cooking evenly, and rotate the dish if needed.
10. Once the bread pudding is cooked through, remove it from the campfire and let it cool slightly before serving.
11. Serve the campfire bread pudding warm, either on its own or topped with a drizzle of maple syrup, caramel sauce, or whipped cream for an extra treat.
12. Enjoy the delicious and comforting flavors of campfire bread pudding as a perfect ending to your outdoor meal!

Feel free to customize your campfire bread pudding by adding extras like chocolate chips, dried fruit, or spices such as nutmeg or cardamom. It's a versatile dessert that's sure to be a hit around the campfire!

Campfire Monkey Bread

Ingredients:

- 2 cans refrigerated biscuit dough (such as Pillsbury Grands)
- 1/2 cup granulated sugar
- 1 teaspoon ground cinnamon
- 1/2 cup unsalted butter
- 1/2 cup brown sugar
- Cooking spray or extra butter for greasing

Instructions:

1. Start by preparing your campfire. You'll want to have a bed of hot coals for cooking.
2. Grease a cast iron skillet or Dutch oven with cooking spray or butter. You can also line the skillet with aluminum foil and grease the foil for easier cleanup.
3. In a small bowl, mix together the granulated sugar and ground cinnamon until well combined.
4. Open the cans of biscuit dough and cut each biscuit into quarters.
5. Roll each biscuit quarter into a ball and then roll it in the cinnamon sugar mixture until coated.
6. Arrange the coated biscuit balls in the greased skillet or Dutch oven.
7. In a small saucepan, melt the butter over the campfire. Once melted, stir in the brown sugar until dissolved and well combined.
8. Pour the butter and brown sugar mixture evenly over the biscuit balls in the skillet or Dutch oven.
9. Cover the skillet or Dutch oven with a lid or aluminum foil.
10. Place the skillet or Dutch oven on the hot coals of the campfire and cook for about 20-30 minutes, or until the monkey bread is golden brown and cooked through.
11. Check the monkey bread occasionally to ensure it's cooking evenly, and rotate the skillet or Dutch oven if needed.
12. Once the monkey bread is cooked through, remove it from the campfire and let it cool slightly before serving.
13. Serve the campfire monkey bread warm, either on its own or with a drizzle of caramel sauce or a scoop of vanilla ice cream for an extra treat.
14. Enjoy the delicious and gooey flavors of campfire monkey bread as a fun and tasty dessert!

Feel free to customize your campfire monkey bread by adding extras like chopped nuts, raisins, or chocolate chips to the biscuit balls before cooking. It's a versatile and crowd-pleasing dessert that's sure to be a hit around the campfire!

Campfire Tacos in a Bag

Ingredients:

- Individual-sized bags of corn chips (such as Doritos or Fritos)
- Cooked taco meat (ground beef, chicken, or turkey seasoned with taco seasoning)
- Shredded lettuce
- Diced tomatoes
- Shredded cheese
- Diced onions (optional)
- Sliced jalapeños (optional)
- Salsa
- Sour cream
- Guacamole or diced avocado (optional)

Instructions:

1. Prepare your campfire. You'll need a cooking grate or a grill with hot coals.
2. Set out the individual bags of corn chips on a flat surface.
3. Prepare the taco meat by cooking ground beef, chicken, or turkey in a skillet over the campfire until browned and cooked through. Season the meat with taco seasoning according to package instructions.
4. Open each bag of corn chips and spoon a generous portion of the cooked taco meat into each bag.
5. Add shredded lettuce, diced tomatoes, shredded cheese, diced onions, sliced jalapeños, salsa, sour cream, and any other desired toppings to each bag.
6. Seal the bags tightly and gently shake or massage them to mix the ingredients together.
7. Carefully open the bags and enjoy your campfire tacos in a bag with a fork or spoon, straight from the bag!

These campfire tacos in a bag are customizable, convenient, and perfect for enjoying outdoors. They're a hit with both kids and adults and make for an easy cleanup since there are no plates required. Feel free to customize the toppings according to your preferences and dietary restrictions.

Campfire Pasta Salad

Ingredients:

- 8 ounces pasta (such as rotini, penne, or bowtie)
- 1 cup cherry tomatoes, halved
- 1/2 cup cucumber, diced
- 1/2 cup bell pepper, diced
- 1/4 cup red onion, finely chopped
- 1/4 cup black olives, sliced
- 1/4 cup feta cheese, crumbled (optional)
- 2 tablespoons fresh parsley, chopped
- Salt and pepper to taste

For the dressing:

- 1/4 cup olive oil
- 2 tablespoons red wine vinegar
- 1 teaspoon Dijon mustard
- 1 clove garlic, minced
- 1/2 teaspoon dried oregano
- Salt and pepper to taste

Instructions:

1. Start by preparing your campfire. You'll want to have a pot of boiling water ready for cooking the pasta.
2. Cook the pasta according to package instructions until al dente. Drain the pasta and rinse it under cold water to stop the cooking process. Set aside to cool.
3. In a large bowl, combine the cooked pasta with the cherry tomatoes, cucumber, bell pepper, red onion, black olives, feta cheese (if using), and fresh parsley.
4. In a small bowl, whisk together the olive oil, red wine vinegar, Dijon mustard, minced garlic, dried oregano, salt, and pepper to make the dressing.
5. Pour the dressing over the pasta salad and toss until everything is evenly coated.
6. Taste the pasta salad and adjust the seasoning with salt and pepper if needed.
7. Cover the bowl with plastic wrap or a lid and refrigerate for at least 30 minutes to allow the flavors to meld together.
8. Once chilled, give the pasta salad a final toss and transfer it to a serving bowl.

9. Serve the campfire pasta salad cold or at room temperature, and enjoy as a delicious side dish or light meal during your outdoor adventure!

Feel free to customize your campfire pasta salad by adding other vegetables, herbs, or proteins according to your taste preferences. It's a versatile dish that's perfect for using up any ingredients you have on hand while camping or enjoying a picnic.

Campfire Caesar Salad

Ingredients:

For the dressing:

- 1/2 cup mayonnaise
- 2 cloves garlic, minced
- 2 tablespoons lemon juice
- 1 tablespoon Dijon mustard
- 2 anchovy fillets, minced (optional)
- 1/4 cup grated Parmesan cheese
- Salt and pepper to taste

For the salad:

- 1 head romaine lettuce, washed and chopped
- 1 cup croutons
- 1/4 cup grated Parmesan cheese
- Optional: grilled chicken breast or shrimp for added protein

Instructions:

1. Start by preparing your campfire. You'll want to have a grill or cooking grate set up over hot coals.
2. In a small bowl, whisk together the mayonnaise, minced garlic, lemon juice, Dijon mustard, minced anchovy fillets (if using), and grated Parmesan cheese until well combined. Season with salt and pepper to taste. This is your Caesar dressing.
3. Place the chopped romaine lettuce in a large mixing bowl.
4. Drizzle the Caesar dressing over the lettuce and toss until the lettuce is evenly coated.
5. Add the croutons and grated Parmesan cheese to the bowl, and toss again to combine.
6. If desired, grill chicken breast or shrimp over the campfire until cooked through, and slice or chop them into bite-sized pieces.
7. Add the grilled chicken or shrimp to the salad, if using, and toss to combine.
8. Transfer the Caesar salad to serving plates or bowls.

9. Serve the campfire Caesar salad immediately, and enjoy as a delicious and satisfying meal while dining outdoors!

This campfire Caesar salad is simple to prepare and bursting with flavor. It's perfect for enjoying as a side dish or a light meal during your outdoor adventures. Feel free to customize the salad with additional toppings such as cherry tomatoes, avocado slices, or hard-boiled eggs, according to your preferences.

Campfire Grilled Vegetables

Ingredients:

- Assorted vegetables (such as bell peppers, zucchini, yellow squash, eggplant, onions, mushrooms, cherry tomatoes, asparagus, or any other vegetables of your choice)
- Olive oil
- Salt and pepper
- Optional seasonings: garlic powder, onion powder, Italian seasoning, or your favorite herbs and spices

Instructions:

1. Start by preparing your campfire. You'll want to have a grill or cooking grate set up over hot coals.
2. Wash and prepare the vegetables. For larger vegetables like bell peppers, zucchini, and eggplant, slice them into even-sized pieces. For smaller vegetables like cherry tomatoes and mushrooms, you can leave them whole or halve them if they're large.
3. Place the prepared vegetables in a large mixing bowl.
4. Drizzle the vegetables with olive oil, using enough to lightly coat them. Season with salt, pepper, and any optional seasonings or herbs/spices of your choice. Toss the vegetables until they are evenly coated with the oil and seasonings.
5. Thread the vegetables onto skewers, alternating different types of vegetables if desired. If using wooden skewers, be sure to soak them in water for at least 30 minutes beforehand to prevent them from burning on the grill.
6. Place the vegetable skewers on the grill or cooking grate over the campfire.
7. Cook the vegetables for about 10-15 minutes, turning occasionally, until they are tender and charred on the edges.
8. Once the vegetables are cooked to your liking, remove them from the grill and transfer them to a serving platter.
9. Serve the campfire grilled vegetables hot, as a flavorful and nutritious side dish or accompaniment to grilled meats or other main dishes.

Campfire grilled vegetables are versatile and can be customized with your favorite vegetables and seasonings. They're perfect for enjoying while camping, picnicking, or simply dining outdoors in the fresh air.

Campfire Sausage and Egg Breakfast Burritos

Ingredients:

- 1 pound breakfast sausage (pork, turkey, or chicken)
- 8 large eggs
- Salt and pepper to taste
- 1 cup shredded cheese (cheddar, Monterey Jack, or your favorite)
- 8 large flour tortillas
- Optional toppings: salsa, diced tomatoes, diced onions, sliced avocado, sour cream, hot sauce

Instructions:

1. Start by preparing your campfire. You'll want to have a grill or cooking grate set up over hot coals.
2. In a skillet or cast iron pan, cook the breakfast sausage over the campfire until browned and cooked through, breaking it up into smaller pieces with a spatula as it cooks. Remove the cooked sausage from the skillet and set it aside.
3. In the same skillet, crack the eggs and scramble them until they are fully cooked. Season with salt and pepper to taste.
4. Once the eggs are cooked, add the cooked sausage back to the skillet and stir to combine.
5. Lay out the flour tortillas on a flat surface. Divide the sausage and egg mixture evenly among the tortillas, placing it in the center of each tortilla.
6. Sprinkle shredded cheese over the sausage and egg mixture on each tortilla.
7. Optional: Add any additional toppings you desire, such as salsa, diced tomatoes, diced onions, sliced avocado, sour cream, or hot sauce.
8. Fold the sides of each tortilla in towards the center, then roll it up tightly to form a burrito.
9. Wrap each burrito individually in aluminum foil.
10. Place the foil-wrapped burritos on the grill or cooking grate over the campfire. Cook for about 5-10 minutes, turning occasionally, until the burritos are heated through and the cheese is melted.
11. Once the burritos are heated through, carefully remove them from the grill and let them cool slightly before serving.
12. Unwrap the foil and serve the campfire sausage and egg breakfast burritos hot, and enjoy a delicious and hearty breakfast to start your day outdoors!

These campfire breakfast burritos are customizable, so feel free to add or substitute ingredients based on your preferences. They're perfect for enjoying while camping, hiking, or just relaxing in nature.

Campfire Chicken and Rice Casserole

Ingredients:

- 1 pound boneless, skinless chicken breasts, cut into bite-sized pieces
- 1 cup long-grain white rice
- 2 cups chicken broth
- 1 cup diced bell peppers (any color)
- 1 cup diced onions
- 1 cup diced carrots
- 1 cup frozen peas
- 2 cloves garlic, minced
- 1 teaspoon dried thyme
- 1 teaspoon dried rosemary
- Salt and pepper to taste
- 1 cup shredded cheese (cheddar, Monterey Jack, or your favorite)

Instructions:

1. Start by preparing your campfire. You'll want to have a bed of hot coals for cooking.
2. In a large cast iron skillet or Dutch oven, combine the chicken pieces, rice, chicken broth, diced bell peppers, onions, carrots, peas, minced garlic, dried thyme, dried rosemary, salt, and pepper. Stir until everything is evenly distributed.
3. Cover the skillet or Dutch oven with a lid or aluminum foil.
4. Place the skillet or Dutch oven on the hot coals of the campfire. Cook for about 30-40 minutes, or until the chicken is cooked through, the rice is tender, and most of the liquid has been absorbed. Stir occasionally to prevent sticking.
5. Once the chicken and rice are cooked, remove the skillet or Dutch oven from the campfire.
6. Sprinkle shredded cheese over the top of the chicken and rice mixture.
7. Cover the skillet or Dutch oven again and let it sit for a few minutes, allowing the cheese to melt.
8. Once the cheese is melted, remove the lid or aluminum foil and serve the campfire chicken and rice casserole hot.
9. Enjoy your delicious and comforting campfire meal!

This campfire chicken and rice casserole is a hearty and satisfying dish that's perfect for outdoor cooking. Feel free to customize it with your favorite vegetables or seasonings. It's a great option for camping trips, picnics, or backyard cookouts!

www.ingramcontent.com/pod-product-compliance
Lightning Source LLC
LaVergne TN
LVHW081612060526
838201LV00054B/2216